To:

_____

From:

_____

Date:

_____

© 2013 Ellie Claire® Gift & Paper Expressions
Franklin, TN 37067
EllieClaire.com
Ellie Claire is a registered trademark of Worthy Media, Inc.

For I Know the PLANS I Have for You (Butterfly)
A *Pocket Inspirations* Book
© 2013 Ellie Claire
Published by Ellie Claire, an imprint of Worthy Publishing Group,
a division of Worthy Media, Inc.

ISBN 978-1-60936-124-2

Compiled by Marilyn Jansen
Designed by Lisa and Jeff Franke

Stock or custom editions of Ellie Claire titles may be purchased in bulk for
educational, business, ministry, fundraising, or sales promotional use. For
information, please e-mail info@ellieclaire.com.

Printed in USA.

For I know
the PLANS I have
for YOU.

JEREMIAH 29:11

Pi Pocket
INSPIRATIONS

Ellie Claire

...inspired by life

Contents

A Bright Future

Your future is as bright as the promises of God.

A. Judson

No eye has seen, no ear has heard, and no mind has
imagined what God has prepared for those who love him.

1 Corinthians 2:9 NLT

What we feel, think, and do this moment influences
both our present and the future in ways we may
never know. Begin. Start right where you are.
Consider your possibilities and find inspiration...
to add more meaning and zest to your life.

Alexandra Stoddard

Commit to the LORD whatever you do,
and your plans will succeed.

Proverbs 16:3 NIV

The future lies before you like a field of driven snow,
Be careful how you tread it, for every step will show.

The path of the virtuous leads away from evil;
whoever follows that path is safe.

Proverbs 16:17 NLT

God has designs on our future...and He has
designed us for the future. He has given us something
to do in the future that no one else can do.

Ruth Senter

"For I know the plans I have for you,"
declares the LORD, "plans to prosper you and not
to harm you, plans to give you hope and a future."

Jeremiah 29:11 NIV

Beauty

A woman of beauty...knows in her quiet center
where God dwells that He finds her beautiful,
and deems her worthy, and in Him, she is enough.

John and Stasi Eldredge

Don't be concerned about the outward beauty of fancy
hairstyles, expensive jewelry, or beautiful clothes.
You should clothe yourselves instead with the beauty
that comes from within, the unfading beauty of a gentle
and quiet spirit, which is so precious to God.

1 Peter 3:3-4 NLT

Your looks at this age are a gift. You received them
from your ancestors. But if you are still beautiful
when your hair is gray and your bones ache,
that beauty is from your own doing.

My cup brims with blessing.
Your beauty and love chase after me
every day of my life.

Psalm 23:5-6 MSG

We do not want merely to see beauty, though,
God knows, even that is bounty enough. We want
something else which can hardly be put into words—
to be united with the beauty we see, to pass into it,
to receive it into ourselves.

C. S. Lewis

I'm asking GOD for one thing, only one thing:
To live with him in his house my whole life long.
I'll contemplate his beauty; I'll study at his feet.
That's the only quiet, secure place in a noisy world.

Psalm 27:4-5 MSG

Dreams and Goals

There is nothing like a dream to create the future.

Victor Hugo

Hope deferred makes the heart sick,
but a dream fulfilled is a tree of life.

Proverb 13:12 NLT

A dream becomes a goal when action
is taken toward its achievement.

Bo Bennett

Dear brothers and sisters, I have not achieved it,
but I focus on this one thing: Forgetting the past and
looking forward to what lies ahead, I press on to reach
the end of the race and receive the heavenly prize for
which God, through Christ Jesus, is calling us.

Philippians 3:13-14 NLT

Shoot for the moon. Even if you miss,
you'll land among the stars.

Les Brown

Every good action and every perfect gift
is from God. These good gifts come down from
the Creator of the sun, moon, and stars, who does
not change like their shifting shadows.

James 1:17 NCV

Nothing is as real as a dream.
The world can change around you, but your
dream will not. Responsibilities need not
erase it. Duties need not obscure it. Because the dream is
within you, no one can take it away.

Tom Clancy

There is surely a future hope for you,
and your hope will not be cut off.

Proverbs 23:18 NIV

Go confidently in the direction of your dreams.
Live the life you have imagined.

Henry David Thoreau

Have Compassion

Society needs people who...know how to be
compassionate and honest.... You can't run
the society on data and computers alone.

Alvin Toffler

What happens when we live God's way?
He brings gifts into our lives...things like affection
for others, exuberance about life...a sense of
compassion in the heart, and a conviction that
a basic holiness permeates things and people.

Galatians 5:22-23 MSG

For the LORD comforts his people and will
have compassion on his afflicted ones.

Isaiah 49:13 NIV

Praise be to the God and Father of our Lord
Jesus Christ, the Father of compassion and the God
of all comfort, who comforts us in all our troubles,
so that we can comfort those in any trouble with the
comfort we ourselves have received from God.

2 Corinthians 1:3-4 NIV

There never was any heart truly great and generous,
that was not also tender and compassionate.

Robert South

Be agreeable, be sympathetic, be loving,
be compassionate, be humble. That goes for all of you,
no exceptions. No retaliation. No sharp-tongued sarcasm.
Instead, bless—that's your job, to bless.
You'll be a blessing and also get a blessing.

1 Peter 3:8-9 MSG

The compassionate person feels with God's heart.

Friends

If you have a gift for showing kindness to others, do it gladly. Don't just pretend to love others. Really love them.

Romans 12:8-9 NLT

Inasmuch as anyone pushes you nearer to God,
he or she is your friend.

It is good and pleasant when God's
people live together in peace!

Psalm 133:1 NCV

Do you want to be wise? Choose wise friends.

Charles Swindoll

A sweet friendship refreshes the soul.

Proverbs 27:9 MSG

A friend is a person with a sneaky knack
of saying good things about you behind your back.

Marilyn Jansen

Encourage one another and build up one another,
just as you also are doing.

1 Thessalonians 5:11 NASB

When you listen to your friends, when you encourage
them, when you do things their way (at least sometimes),
you're really telling them, "I'm glad you're my friend."

Emilie Barnes

Love one another fervently with a pure heart.

1 Peter 1:22 NKJV

There are high spots in all of our lives, and most of them
come about through encouragement from someone else.

George Adams

The Road Ahead

My Lord God, I have no idea where I am going.
I do not see the road ahead of me. I cannot know for
certain where it will end.... But I believe that the desire
to please You does in fact please You. And I hope I
have that desire in all that I am doing. I hope that I will
never do anything apart from that desire. And I know
that if I do this, You will lead me by the right road
though I may know nothing about it.
Therefore will I trust You always, though I may seem
to be lost and in the shadow of death. I will not fear,
for You are ever with me. And You will never leave
me to face my perils alone.

Thomas Merton

I would rather walk with God in the dark
than go alone in the light.

Mary Gardiner Brainard

You are a chosen people, a royal priesthood,
a holy nation, a people belonging to God,
that you may declare the praises of him who called
you out of darkness into his wonderful light.

1 Peter 2:9 NIV

Heaven often seems distant and unknown,
but if He who made the road...is our guide,
we need not fear to lose the way.

Henry van Dyke

*I am always with you;
you hold me by my right hand.*

Psalm 73:23 NIV

Promise of Love

A rainbow stretches from one end of the sky
to the other. Each shade of color, each facet of
light displays the radiant spectrum of God's love.
It can remind us that He will always love each
one of us at our worst and at our best.

Faithful, O Lord, Thy mercies are,
A rock that cannot move!
A thousand promises declare
Thy constancy of love.

Charles Wesley

May your unfailing love come to me, O LORD,
your salvation according to your promise.

Psalm 119:41 NIV

God's love never ceases. Never.... God doesn't love us less
if we fail or more if we succeed. God's love never ceases.

Max Lucado

*𝒢OD promises to love me all day, sing songs
all through the night! My life is God's prayer.*

Psalm 42:8 MSG

God has not promised sun without rain,
Joy without sorrow, peace without pain.
But God has promised strength for the day,
Rest for the labor, light for the way,
Grace for the trials, help from above,
Unfailing sympathy, undying love.

Annie Johnson Flint

God makes a promise—faith believes it,
hope anticipates it, patience quietly awaits it.

Stay Focused

Many an opportunity is lost because one
is out looking for four-leaf clovers.

Let us not grow weary while doing good, for in due
season we shall reap if we do not lose heart. Therefore,
as we have opportunity, let us do good to all.

Galatians 6:7–10 NKJV

Goals provide the energy source that powers our lives.
One of the best ways we can get the most from
the energy we have is to focus it. That is what goals
can do for us; concentrate our energy.

Denis Waitley

I'm not saying that I have this all together, that I have it
made. But I am well on my way, reaching out for Christ,
who has so wondrously reached out for me.

Philippians 3:12 MSG

All who have accomplished great things have had a great aim, have fixed their gaze on a goal which was high, one which sometimes seemed impossible.

Orison Swett Marden

Look straight ahead, and fix your eyes on what lies before you.
Mark out a straight path for your feet;
stay on the safe path.
Don't get sidetracked; keep your feet from following evil.

Proverbs 4:25–27 NLT

We need a focus. A main thing. Something bigger than skin cream or tennis shoes that remind us of the purpose of it all. If we expect to regain a more simple heart, a more centered pace for our day, we need to order our lives in specific ways.

David and Barbara Sorensen

God's Care

The LORD is my shepherd; I shall not want.
He makes me to lie down in green pastures;
He leads me beside the still waters. He restores
my soul; He leads me in the paths of righteousness
for His name's sake. Yea, thought I walk through
the alley of the shadow of death, I will fear no evil;
for You are with me; Your rod and Your staff,
they comfort me. You prepare a table before
me in the presence of my enemies.

Psalm 23:1-5 NKJV

God never abandons anyone on whom He
has set His love; nor does Christ, the good shepherd,
ever lose track of His sheep.

J. I. Packer

*If God cares so wonderfully for
wildflowers that are here today
and thrown into the fire tomorrow,
he will certainly care for you.*

Matthew 6:30 NLT

God cares for the world He created, from
the rising of a nation to the falling of the
sparrow. Everything in the world lies under the
watchful gaze of His providential eyes, from
the numbering of the days of our life to the
numbering of the hairs on our head. When
we look at the world from that perspective, it
produces within us a response of reverence.

Ken Gire

A Work of Art

Each one of us is God's special work of art.
Through us, He teaches and inspires, delights and
encourages, informs and uplifts all those who view our
lives. God, the master artist, is most concerned about
expressing Himself—His thoughts and His intentions—
through what He paints in our character.... [He] wants
to paint a beautiful portrait of His Son in and through
your life. A painting like no other in all of time.

Joni Eareckson Tada

*I will give thanks to You, for I am fearfully
and wonderfully made; wonderful are Your works,
and my soul knows it very well.*

Psalm 139:14 NASB

Whether we are poets or parents or teachers or artists or
gardeners, we must start where we are and use what we
have. In the process of creation and relationship, what
seems mundane and trivial may show itself to be holy,
precious, part of a pattern.

Luci Shaw

Hold on to the pattern of wholesome teaching you
learned from me—a pattern shaped by the faith and love
that you have in Christ Jesus.

2 Timothy 1:13 NLT

Beauty puts a face on God. When we gaze at nature,
at a loved one, at a work of art, our soul immediately
recognizes and is drawn to the face of God.

Margaret Brownley

The Road

You have brains in your head. You have feet in your shoes.
You can steer yourself in any direction you choose.
You're on your own. And you know what you know.
You are the [one] who'll decide where to go.

Dr. Seuss

The LORD directs the steps of the godly.
He delights in every detail of their lives.
Though they stumble, they will never fall,
for the LORD holds them by the hand.

Psalm 37:23–24 NLT

God, who has led you safely on so far, will lead you on to
the end. Be altogether at rest in the loving holy confidence
which you ought to have in His heavenly providence.

Francis de Sales

From now on every road you travel
Will take you to GOD.
Follow the Covenant signs;
Read the charted directions.

Psalm 25:10 MSG

We may not all reach God's ideal for us, but with
His help we may move in that direction day by
day as we relate every detail of our lives to Him.

In all your ways acknowledge Him,
And He shall direct your paths.

Proverbs 3:6 NKJV

My Help

I will lift up my eyes to the mountains; from where shall
my help come? My help comes from the LORD, who made
heaven and earth. He will not allow your foot to slip;
He who keeps you will not slumber. Behold, He who
keeps Israel will neither slumber nor sleep. The LORD is
your keeper; the LORD is your shade on your right hand.
The sun will not smite you by day, nor the moon
by night. The LORD will protect you from all evil;
He will keep your soul. The LORD will guard your going
out and your coming in from this time forth and forever.

Psalm 121:1-8 NASB

Whatever God tells us to do, He also helps us to do.

Dora Greenwell

We have a Father in heaven who is almighty,
who loves His children as He loves His only-begotten Son,
and whose very joy and delight it is to...help them
at all times and under all circumstances.

George Mueller

*GOD's strong name is our help,
the same GOD who made heaven and earth.*

Psalm 124:8 MSG

When we pray we should keep in mind all of the
shortcomings and excesses we feel, and pour them out
freely to God, our faithful Father, who is ready to help.

Martin Luther

Today Is Unique

Every day we live is a priceless gift of God,
loaded with possibilities to learn something new,
to gain fresh insights.

Dale Evans Rogers

This is the day the LORD has made;
we will rejoice and be glad in it.

Psalm 118:24 NKJV

*Today is unique! It has never occurred
before and it will never be repeated. At midnight
it will end, quietly, suddenly, totally. Forever.
But the hours between now and then are
opportunities with eternal possibilities.*

Charles R. Swindoll

I will bless the LORD at all times;
His praise shall continually be in my mouth.

Psalm 34:1 NKJV

Time is a very precious gift of God; so precious
that it's only given to us moment by moment.

Amelia Barr

Go after a life of love as if your life depended on it—
because it does. Give yourselves to the gifts God gives
you. Most of all, try to proclaim his truth.

1 Corinthians 14:1 MSG

Each day offers time to draw closer to God
and take new steps toward living with purpose.

Be careful how you live.... Make the most
of every opportunity.... Don't act thoughtlessly,
but understand what the Lord wants you to do.

Ephesians 5:15-17 NLT

The Bright Side

Try to keep your sense of humor! When you can
see the funny side of a problem, sometimes it stops
being so much of a problem.

Emilie Barnes

And now, GOD, do it again—
bring rains to our drought-stricken lives....
So those who went off with heavy hearts
will come home laughing, with armloads of blessing.

Psalm 126:4–6 MSG

Keep your face to the sunshine
and you cannot see the shadow.

Helen Keller

The ways of right-living people glow with light;
the longer they live, the brighter they shine.

Proverbs 4:18 MSG

*It never hurts your eyesight to look
on the bright side of things.*

Barbara Johnson

In this world you will have trouble. But take heart!
I have overcome the world.

John 16:33 NIV

When I'm stressed I think of my friends and
how much they love me. Then I feel better.

Jasmine J.

Laugh with your happy friends when they're happy.

Romans 12:15 MSG

It is pleasing to God whenever you rejoice
or laugh from the bottom of your heart.

Martin Luther

Seeds

Don't judge each day by the harvest you reap
but by the seeds that you plant.

Robert Louis Stevenson

Plant your seed in the morning and keep busy all
afternoon, for you don't know if profit will come from
one activity or another—or maybe both.

Ecclesiastes 11:6 NLT

I will consider my earthly existence to have been
wasted unless I can recall a loving family,
a consistent investment in the lives of people,
and an earnest attempt to serve the God who made me.

James Dobson

It's not important who does the planting, or who does the watering. What's important is that God makes the seed grow. The one who plants and the one who waters work together with the same purpose. And both will be rewarded.

1 Corinthians 3:7-8 NLT

The true meaning of life is to plant trees,
under whose shade you do not expect to sit.

Nelson Henderson

When you're kind to others, you help yourself;
when you're cruel to others, you hurt yourself.

Proverbs 11:17 MSG

Bright Dreams

No matter what your age or your situation,
your dreams are achievable. Whether you're five or 105,
you have a lifetime ahead of you!

Oh, how sweet the light of day, and how
wonderful to live in the sunshine! Even if you live
a long time, don't take a single day for granted.
Take delight in each light-filled hour.

Ecclesiastes 11:7-8 MSG

A #2 pencil and a dream can take you anywhere.

Joyce Meyer

Toss your faded dreams not into a trash bin
but into a drawer where you are likely
to rummage some bright morning.

Robert Brault

*The important thing really is not the deed
well done or the medal that you possess, but the
dedication and dreams out of which they grow.*

Robert H. Benson

Steep your life in God-reality, God-initiative,
God-provisions. Don't worry about missing out.
You'll find all your everyday human concerns will be met.

Matthew 6:33 MSG

The victory of success is half won when one gains
the habit of setting goals and achieving them.
Even the most tedious chore will become endurable
as you parade through each day convinced that
every task, no matter how menial or boring,
brings you closer to fulfilling your dreams.

Og Mandino

When You Talk

Let everything you say be good and helpful,
so that your words will be an encouragement
to those who hear them.

Ephesians 4:29 NLT

*When you talk, choose the very same words
that you would use if Jesus were looking
over your shoulder. Because He is.*

Marie T. Freeman

The mouth speaks out of that which fills the heart.

Matthew 12:34 NASB

There's an opportune time to do things,
a right time for everything on the earth....
A right time to shut up and another to speak up.

Ecclesiastes 3:1, 7 MSG

A little kindly advice is better than
a great deal of scolding.

Fanny Crosby

Kind words are like honey—
sweet to the soul and healthy for the body.

Proverbs 16:24 NLT

Everyone should be quick to listen,
slow to speak and slow to become angry.

James 1:17 NIV

A friend understands what you are trying to say...even
when your thoughts aren't fitting into words.

Ann D. Parrish

May the words of my mouth
and the meditation of my heart
be pleasing to you,
O LORD, my rock and my redeemer.

Psalm 19:14 NLT

His Beautiful World

Forbid that I should walk through
Thy beautiful world with unseeing eyes:
Forbid that the lure of the market-place should ever
entirely steal my heart away from
the love of the open acres and the green trees:
Forbid that under the low roof of workshop or office or
study I should ever forget Thy great overarching sky.

John Baillie

Yet God has made everything beautiful for its own time. He has planted eternity in the human heart, but even so, people cannot see the whole scope of God's work from beginning to end.

Ecclesiastes 3:11 NLT

If God hath made this world so fair...
How beautiful beyond compare
Will paradise be found!

James Montgomery

The whole earth is full of His glory!

Isaiah 6:3 NKJV

Our Creator would never have made such lovely days,
and given us the deep hearts to enjoy them, above and
beyond all thought, unless we were meant to be immortal.

Nathaniel Hawthorne

May God give you eyes to see beauty
only the heart can understand.

Learn It All

Get over the idea that only children should spend their
time in study. Be a student so long as you still have
something to learn, and this will mean all your life.

Henry L. Doherty

I'm asking God for one thing, only one thing:
To live with Him in His house my whole life long....
I'll study at His feet.

Psalm 27:4 MSG

It's what you learn after you know it all that counts.

Harry S. Truman

*Let the wise listen and add to their learning,
and let the discerning get guidance.*

Proverbs 1:5 NIV

A study of the nature and character of God
is the most practical project anyone can engage in.
Knowing about God is crucially important
for the living of our lives.

J. I. Packer

Continue in what you have learned and have become
convinced of, because you know those from whom
you learned it, and how from infancy you have
known the holy Scriptures, which are able to make
you wise for salvation through faith in Christ Jesus.

2 Timothy 3:14-15 NIV

A single conversation across the table with a wise
person is worth a month's study of books.

Chinese Proverb

Greater Love

Clothe yourselves with compassion, kindness,
humility, gentleness and patience. Bear with each
other and forgive whatever grievances you may have
against one another. Forgive as the Lord forgave you.
And over all these virtues put on love, which binds
them all together in perfect unity.

Colossians 3:12–14 NIV

What reveals a genuine love for God is my ability to
convince my family and others of my love for them.

Jack Frost

Serve each other with love. The whole law
is made complete in this one command:
"Love your neighbor as you love yourself."

Galatians 5:13–14 NCV

Love must be sincere.... Honor one another
above yourselves.

Romans 12:7-10 NIV

*This is My commandment, that you love
one another, just as I have loved you.
Greater love has no one than this,
that one lay down his life for his friends.*

John 15:12-13 NASB

In God's wisdom, He frequently chooses
to meet our needs by showing His love toward
us through the hands and hearts of others.

Jack Hayford

Be kind and compassionate to one another,
forgiving each other, just as in Christ God forgave you.

Ephesians 4:32 NIV

Step of Faith

Don't be afraid to take a big step if one is indicated;
you can't cross a chasm in two small jumps.

David Lloyd George

You took a risk trusting Me, and now you're
healed and whole. Live well, live blessed!

Luke 8:48 MSG

When you come to the end of all the light
you know, and it's time to step into the darkness
of the unknown, faith is knowing that one of two
things shall happen: Either you will be given something
solid to stand on or you will be taught to fly.

Edward Teller

𝓕or we walk by faith, not by sight.

2 Corinthians 5:7 NKJV

Optimism is the faith that leads to achievement.
Nothing can be done without hope and confidence.

Helen Keller

Be strong and let your heart take courage,
All you who hope in the LORD.

Psalm 31:24 NASB

From the little spark may burst a mighty flame.

Dante

May He give you the power to accomplish
all the good things your faith prompts you to do.

2 Thessalonians 1:11 NLT

Make the Best

Achievement is the knowledge that you have studied
and worked hard and done the best that is in you.
Success is being praised by others, and that's nice, too,
but not as important or satisfying. Always aim for
achievement and forget about success.

Helen Hayes

May He grant you according to your heart's desire,
And fulfill all your purpose.

Psalm 20:4 NKJV

Hope, in this deep and powerful sense, is not the same
as joy that things are going well, or willingness to invest
in enterprises that are obviously heading for success, but
rather an ability to work for something because it is good.

Václav Havel

You were taught, with regard to your former
way of life, to put off your old self...to be made
new in the attitude of your minds.

Ephesians 4:22–23 NIV

*Things turn out best for the people who
make the best out of the way things turn out.*

Art Linkletter

Common sense is the measure of the possible;
it is composed of experience and prevision;
it is calculation applied to life.

Henri Frédéric Amiel

The price of success is hard work, dedication to the job at
hand, and the determination that whether we win or lose,
we have applied the best of ourselves to the task at hand.

Vincent T. Lombardi

Totally Aware

God is every moment totally aware of each one of us.
Totally aware in intense concentration and love....
No one passes through any area of life, happy or tragic,
without the attention of God with them.

Eugenia Price

GOD takes care of all who stay close to him

Psalm 31:23 MSG

Because God is responsible for our welfare, we are told
to cast all our care upon Him, for He cares for us.
God says, "I'll take the burden—don't give it a
thought—leave it to Me." God is keenly aware that
we are dependent upon Him for life's necessities.

Billy Graham

I lay down and slept,
yet I woke up in safety,
for the LORD was watching over me.

Psalm 3:5 NLT

You are God's created beauty and the focus
of His affection and delight.

Janet L. Smith

Live carefree before God; he is most careful with you.

1 Peter 5:7 MSG

*From the tiny birds of the air and from the
fragile lilies of the field we learn the same truth,
which is so important for those who desire a life
of simple faith: God takes care of His own.
He knows our needs. He anticipates our crises.*

Charles Swindoll

Freely Share

You can't live a perfect day without doing something
for someone who will never be able to repay you.

John Wooden

Each of you has received a gift to use to serve others.
Be good servants of God's various gifts of grace.

1 Peter 4:10 NCV

Giving is a joy if we do it in the right spirit.
It all depends on whether we think of it as
"What can I spare?" or as "What can I share?"

Esther York Burkholder

Those who will use their skill and constructive
imagination to see how much they can give for a dollar,
instead of how little they can give for a dollar,
are bound to succeed.

Henry Ford

*This service you do not only helps
the needs of God's people, it also brings many
more thanks to God. It is a proof of your faith.
Many people will praise God because you
obey the Good News...and because you freely
share with them and with all others.*

2 Corinthians 9:12 – 13 NCV

The secret of life is that all we have
and are is a gift of grace to be shared.

Lloyd John Ogilvie

Remind the people...to be ready to do whatever
is good,...to be peaceable and considerate,
and to show true humility toward all men.

Titus 3:1 – 2 NIV

Learn More

You learn something every day if you pay attention.

Roy LeBlond

Pay close attention, friend, to what your father
tells you; never forget what you learned at your
mother's knee. Wear their counsel like flowers
in your hair, like rings on your fingers.

Proverbs 1:8–9 MSG

The purpose of learning is growth, and our minds, unlike
our bodies, can continue growing as we continue to live.

Mortimer Adler

*The mind of a person with understanding gets
knowledge; the wise person listens to learn more.*

Proverbs 18:15 NCV

I am defeated, and know it, if I meet any human being
from whom I find myself unable to learn anything.

George Herbert Palmer

Teach the wise, and they will become even wiser;
teach good people, and they will learn even more.

Proverbs 9:9 NCV

No matter how some may think themselves accomplished,
when they set out to learn a new language, science,
or the bicycle, they have entered a new realm as truly
as if they were a child newly born into the world.

Frances Willard

Don't copy the behavior and customs of this world,
but let God transform you into a new person by changing
the way you think. Then you will learn to know God's
will for you, which is good and pleasing and perfect.

Romans 12:2 NLT

Divine Romance

Get into the habit of saying, "Speak, Lord,"
and life will become a romance.

Oswald Chambers

*To fall in love with God is the greatest
of all romances—to seek Him the
greatest of all adventures, to find Him the
greatest human achievement.*

Augustine

Nothing in all creation will ever be able to separate us
from the love of God.

Romans 8:39 NLT

God's love is like a river springing up in the Divine
Substance and flowing endlessly through His creation,
filling all things with life and goodness and strength.

Thomas Merton

He brought me to the banqueting house,
and his banner over me was love.

Song of Solomon 2:4 NKJV

Love Him totally who gave Himself totally for your love.

Clare of Assisi

We know how much God loves us, and we have
put our trust in his love. God is love, and all who
live in love live in God, and God lives in them.

1 John 4:16 NLT

God's holy beauty comes near you, like a spiritual scent,
and it stirs your drowsing soul.... He creates in you
the desire to find Him and run after Him—to follow
wherever He leads you, and to press peacefully against
His heart wherever He is. If you are seeking after God,
you may be sure of this: God is seeking you
much more. He is the Lover, and you are His beloved.
He has promised Himself to you.

John of the Cross

Rewarding Work

There's no thrill in easy sailing
when the skies are clear and blue,
There's no joy in merely doing things
which anyone can do.
But there is some satisfaction
that is mighty sweet to take,
when you reach a destination
that you thought you'd never make.

Whenever it is possible, choose some occupation which
you should do even if you did not need the money.

William Lyon Phelps

Work with a smile on your face, always keeping
in mind that no matter who happens to be giving
the orders, you're really serving God.

Ephesians 6:7 MSG

Wise words bring many benefits,
and hard work brings rewards.

Proverbs 12:14 NLT

Beauty is also to be found in a day's work.

Mamie Sypert Burns

My heart rejoiced in all my labor;
And this was my reward from all my labor.

Ecclesiastes 2:10 NKJV

The secret of joy in work is contained
in one word—excellence. To know how
to do something well is to enjoy it.

Pearl S. Buck

Therefore, my beloved brethren, be steadfast,
immovable, always abounding in the work of the Lord,
knowing that your labor is not in vain in the Lord.

1 Corinthians 15:58 NKJV

Dare to Dream

Your righteousness, O God, reaches to the highest heavens.
You have done such wonderful things.
Who can compare with you, O God?

Psalm 71:17 NLT

*You can't experience success beyond
your wildest dreams until you dare
to dream something wild!*

Scott Sorrell

God can do anything, you know—far more than you could
ever imagine or guess or request in your wildest dreams!

Ephesians 3:20 MSG

Somehow I can't believe that there are any
heights that can't be scaled by a person who
knows the secrets of making dreams come true.
This special secret...can be summarized in four Cs.
They are curiosity, confidence, courage, and constancy.

Walt Disney

My child, eat honey, for it is good, and the honeycomb is sweet to the taste. In the same way, wisdom is sweet to your soul. If you find it, you will have a bright future, and your hopes will not be cut short.

Proverbs 24:13-14 NLT

One hundred years from today your present income will be inconsequential. One hundred years from now it won't matter if you got that big break, took the trip to Europe, or finally traded up to a Mercedes.... It will matter that you knew God.

David Sibley

Dear friend, listen well to my words.... Those who discover these words live, really live; body and soul.... Keep vigilant watch over your heart; that's where life starts.

Proverbs 4:20-23 MSG

Yourself

Make the most of yourself, for that is all there is of you.

Ralph Waldo Emerson

Be wise in the way you act...make the most
of every opportunity. Let your conversation
be always full of grace, seasoned with salt,
so that you may know how to answer everyone.

Colossians 4:5-6 NIV

*The golden opportunity you are seeking
is in yourself. It is not in your environment;
it is not in luck or chance, or the help of others;
it is in yourself alone.*

Orison Swett Marden

So, friends, confirm God's invitation to you,
his choice of you. Don't put it off; do it now.
Do this, and you'll have your life on a firm footing.

2 Peter 1:10-11 MSG

The most important person to be honest with is yourself.

Becoming a leader is synonymous with becoming yourself.
It is precisely that simple, and it is also that difficult.

Warren G. Bennis

Anyone who belongs to Christ
has become a new person.
The old life is gone; a new life has begun!
And all of this is a gift from God.

1 Corinthians 5:17-18 NLT

Immeasurable Love

We are so preciously loved by God that we cannot
even comprehend it. No created being can ever
know how much and how sweetly and tenderly God
loves them. It is only with the help of His grace
that we are able to persevere in...endless wonder
at the high, surpassing, immeasurable love which
our Lord in His goodness has for us.

Julian of Norwich

I have loved you with an everlasting love;
I have drawn you with loving-kindness.

Jeremiah 31:3 NIV

If you have a special need today, focus your full
attention on the goodness and greatness of your
Father rather than on the size of your need. Your need
is so small compared to His ability to meet it.

God says, "I love you no matter what you do."
His love is unconditional and unending.

Do not dwell upon your inner failings....
Just do this: Bring your soul to the Great Physician—
exactly as you are, even and especially at your
worst moment.... For it is in such moments that you
will most readily sense His healing presence.

Teresa of Avila

Then Christ will make his home in your hearts as you
trust in him. Your roots will grow down into God's
love and keep you strong.

Ephesians 3:17 NLT

Every Need

God wants nothing from us except our needs,
and these furnish Him with room to display His
bounty when He supplies them freely....
Not what I have, but what I do not have,
is the first point of contact between my soul and God.

Charles H. Spurgeon

He himself gives life and breath to everything,
and he satisfies every need.

Acts 17:25 NLT

*Jesus Christ has brought every need,
every joy, every gratitude, every hope of ours
before God. He accompanies us and brings
us into the presence of God.*

Dietrich Bonhoeffer

Do not worry about anything, but pray and ask God for
everything you need, always giving thanks. And God's
peace, which is so great we cannot understand it,
will keep your hearts and minds in Christ Jesus.

Philippians 4:6–7 NCV

The "air" which our souls need also envelops all of
us at all times and on all sides. God is round about us...
on every hand, with many-sided and all-sufficient grace.

Ole Hallesby

My God will supply all your needs according
to His riches in glory in Christ Jesus.

Philippians 4:19 NASB

Wonder and Praise

If you have never heard the mountains singing,
or seen the trees of the field clapping their hands,
do not think because of that they don't.
Ask God to open your ears so you may hear it,
and your eyes so you may see it, because,
though few people ever know it, they do,
my friend, they do.

Phillips McCandlish

who can list the glorious miracles of the LORD?
Who can ever praise him enough?

Psalm 106:2 NLT

The love of the Father is like a sudden rain shower
that will pour forth when you least expect it,
catching you up into wonder and praise.

Richard J. Foster

The wonder of living is held within the beauty
of silence, the glory of sunlight...the sweetness
of fresh spring air, the quiet strength of earth,
and the love that lies at the very root of all things.

The LORD is my strength and my song;
he has become my salvation.
He is my God, and I will praise him,
my father's God, and I will exalt him....
Who is like you—majestic in holiness,
awesome in glory, working wonders?

Exodus 15:2, 11 NIV

Persevere

The difference between perseverance
and obstinacy is that one often comes from
a strong will, and the other from a strong won't.

Henry Ward Beecher

God blesses those who patiently endure
testing and temptation. Afterward they will
receive the crown of life that God has
promised to those who love him.

James 1:12 NLT

Life is not easy for any of us. But what of that?
We must have perseverance and above all confidence
in ourselves. We must believe that we are gifted for
something and that this thing must be attained.

Marie Curie

We are made to persist.
That's how we find out who we are.

Tobias Wolff

And so I tell you, keep on asking, and you will receive
what you ask for. Keep on seeking, and you will find.
Keep on knocking, and the door will be opened to you.

Luke 11:9 NLT

Never, Never, Never Quit.

Winston Churchill

Let us throw off everything that hinders and the sin
that so easily entangles, and let us run with
perseverance the race marked out for us. Let us fix our
eyes on Jesus, the author and perfecter of our faith.

Hebrews 12:1-2 NIV

Always Loved

God loves us for ourselves. He values our love more
than He values galaxies of new created worlds.

A. W. Tozer

If you believe in God, it is not too difficult to believe
that He is concerned about the universe and all the
events on this earth. But the really staggering message
of the Bible is that this same God cares deeply about
you and your identity and the events of your life....
We have missed the full impact of the Gospel if we have
not discovered what it is to be ourselves, loved by God,
irreplaceable in His sight, unique among our fellowmen.

Bruce Larson

I'll never quit telling the story of your love....
Your love has always been our lives' foundation,
your fidelity has been the roof over our world.

Psalm 89:2 MSG

Our greatness rests solely on the fact that God
in His incomprehensible goodness has bestowed His
love upon us. God does not love us because we are so
valuable; we are valuable because God loves us.

Helmut Thielicke

*For GOD is sheer beauty, all-generous in love,
loyal always and ever.*

Psalm 100:5 MSG

Let your faith in Christ, the omnipresent One, be in
the quiet confidence that He will every day and every
moment keep you as the apple of His eye.

Andrew Murray

Get Up and Lead

Leadership is a combination of strategy and character.
If you must be without one, be without the strategy.

H. Norman Schwarzkopf

Love and truth form a good leader; sound leadership is
founded on loving integrity.

Proverbs 20:28 MSG

*In simplest terms, leaders are those who know
where they want to go, and get up, and go.*

John Erskine

Without wise leadership, a nation falls;
there is safety in having many advisers.

Proverbs 11:14 NLT

Real leaders are ordinary people
with extraordinary determination.

Good leaders cultivate honest speech;
they love advisors who tell them the truth.

Proverbs 16:13 MSG

Men make history, and not the other way around. In
periods where there is no leadership, society stands still.
Progress occurs when courageous, skillful leaders seize the
opportunity to change things for the better.

Harry S. Truman

Those who are wise will shine like the brightness of the
heavens, and those who lead many to righteousness, like
the stars for ever and ever.

Daniel 12:3 NIV

When you grow up in an environment where...
commitment and dedication is not just talked about
but lived so fully, so honestly, there is no way
that it does not take root in your being.

Yolanda King

Give Freely

Give, and it will be given to you. A good measure,
pressed down, shaken together and running over,
will be poured into your lap. For with the measure
you use, it will be measured to you.

Luke 6:38 NIV

Wise are those who learn that the bottom line
doesn't always have to be their top priority.

William A. Ward

A good name is to be chosen rather than great riches,
Loving favor rather than silver and gold.

Proverbs 22:1 NKJV

The measure of a life, after all,
is not its duration but its donation.

Corrie ten Boom

Give freely and spontaneously. Don't have a stingy heart. The way you handle matters like this triggers GOD, your God's, blessing in everything you do, all your work and ventures. There are always going to be poor and needy people among you. So I command you: Always be generous, open purse and hands, give to your neighbors in trouble, your poor and hurting neighbors.

Deuteronomy 15:10–11 MSG

Remember, giving is a privilege—not a duty.
Not everyone has enough to give to others.

In everything I did, I showed you that by this
kind of hard work we must help the weak,
remembering the words the Lord Jesus himself said:
"It is more blessed to give than to receive."

Acts 20:35 NIV

Busyness

Don't ever let yourself get so busy that you
miss those little but important extras in life—
the beauty of a day...the smile of a friend....
For it is often life's smallest pleasures and gentlest joys
that make the biggest and most lasting difference.

We are merely moving shadows,
and all our busy rushing ends in nothing.
We heap up wealth,
not knowing who will spend it.
And so, Lord, where do I put my hope?
My only hope is in you.

Psalm 39:6-7 NLT

There are no shortcuts to any place worth going.

Beverly Sills

What kind of deal is it to get everything you want but
lose yourself? What could you ever trade your soul for?

Matthew 16:26 MSG

*The busyness of life has so many of us
trying desperately to fit too many activities
into each day. Experts would tell us that when
we are under stress, we should especially then
make time to exercise. It's all the more true,
for our spiritual and emotional health,
that the last thing we should eliminate from
our schedules is quiet time with the Lord.*

You will experience God's peace, which exceeds
anything we can understand. His peace will guard
your hearts and minds as you live in Christ Jesus.

Philippians 4:7 NLT

O Lord, You know how busy I must be today.
If I forget You, do not You forget me.

Anthony Ashley Cooper

A Pattern of Beauty

I see in the stars, in the rivers, I see in the
open fields, patches of heaven and threads
of paradise. Let me sew the earth, the day, the way
of my life into a pattern that forms a quilt,
God's quilt, to keep me warm today and always.

Christopher de Vinck

"Take your needle, my child, and work at
your pattern; it will come out a rose by and by."
Life is like that; one stitch at a time
taken patiently, and the pattern will come
out all right like embroidery.

Oliver Wendell Holmes

Oh, that my steps might be steady,
keeping to the course you set.... I thank you
for speaking straight from your heart;
I learn the pattern of your righteous ways.

Psalm 119:5, 7 MSG

Even when all we see are the tangled threads
on the backside of life's tapestry, we know that
God is good and is out to do us good always.

Richard J. Foster

Taken separately, the experiences of life can work
harm and not good. Taken together, they make
a pattern of blessing and strength the like
of which the world does not know.

V. Raymond Edman

*The patterns of our days are always changing...
rearranging...and each design for living is unique...
graced with its own special beauty.*

Learn Now

Do you know the difference between education and
experience? Education is when you read the fine print;
experience is what you get when you don't.

Pete Seeger

Those who refuse correction hate themselves,
but those who accept correction gain understanding.
Respect for the Lord will teach you wisdom.
If you want to be honored, you must be humble.

Proverbs 15:32-33 NCV

Learn as much as you can while you are young,
since life becomes too busy later.

Dana Stewart Scott

Do not let anyone treat you as if you are
unimportant because you are young. Instead,
be an example...with your words, your actions,
your love, your faith, and your pure life.

1 Timothy 4:12 NCV

Anyone who stops learning is old,
whether at twenty or eighty.

Henry Ford

Cease listening to instruction...and you will
stray from the words of knowledge.

Proverbs 19:27 NKJV

*We learn more by looking for
the answer to a question...than we do
from learning the answer itself.*

Lloyd Alexander

You will search again for the LORD your God.
And if you search for him with all your
heart and soul, you will find him.

Deuteronomy 4:29 NLT

Different Gifts

Everyone has a unique role to fill in the world
and is important in some respect. Everyone,
including and perhaps especially you, is indispensable.

Nathaniel Hawthorne

*Just as each of us has one body with
many members, and these members do not
all have the same function, so in Christ we
who are many form one body, and each member
belongs to all the others. We have different gifts,
according to the grace given us.*

Romans 12:4-6 NIV

What we are is God's gift to us.
What we become is our gift to God.

Eleanor Powell

For the LORD God is our sun and our shield.
He gives us grace and glory. The LORD will withhold
no good thing from those who do what is right.

Psalm 84:11 NLT

God has a wonderful plan for each person He has
chosen. He knew even before He created this world
what beauty He would bring forth from our lives.

Louise B. Wyly

I pray that from his glorious, unlimited resources he
will empower you with inner strength through his
Spirit. Then Christ will make his home in your hearts
as you trust in him. Your roots will grow down into
God's love and keep you strong.

Ephesians 3:16–17 NLT

Within Your Heart

Never let loyalty and kindness leave you! Tie them
around your neck as a reminder. Write them deep
within your heart. Then you will find favor with both
God and people, and you will earn a good reputation.
Trust in the LORD with all your heart; do not depend
on your own understanding. Seek his will in all you
do, and he will show you which path to take.

Proverbs 3:3-6 NLT

The road to the head lies through the heart.

American Proverb

Learn to love appropriately. You need
to use your head and test your feelings
so that your love is sincere and intelligent.

Philippians 1:9-10 MSG

The riches that are in the heart cannot be stolen.

Russian Proverb

I will give them singleness of heart and put a new
spirit within them. I will take away their stony,
stubborn heart and give them a tender, responsive heart.

Ezekiel 11:19 NLT

*Those who are steadily learning how to love are
enabled to do this because the very love of God,
Himself, has been put into our hearts.*

Eugenia Price

I want them to be strengthened and joined
together with love so that they may be rich
in their understanding. This leads to their knowing
fully God's secret, that is, Christ himself.

Colossians 2:2 NCV

The head learns new things, but the heart
forevermore practices old experiences.

Henry Ward Beecher

Friends Stick Together

Friends are an indispensable part of a meaningful life.
They are the ones who share our burdens and multiply
our blessings. A true friend sticks by us in our joys and
sorrows. In good times and bad, we need friends who will
pray for us, listen to us, and lend a comforting hand and
an understanding ear when needed.

Beverly LaHaye

Bring bread to the table and your friends
will bring their joy to share.

French Proverb

*There are "friends" who destroy each other,
but a real friend sticks closer than a brother.*

Proverbs 18:24 NLT

A friend is somebody who loves us
with understanding, as well as emotion.

Robert Louis Stevenson

An open rebuke
is better than hidden love!
Wounds from a sincere friend
are better than many kisses from an enemy.

Proverbs 27:5–6 NLT

Hold a true friend with both your hands.

Nigerian Proverb

One of life's greatest treasures is the love
that binds hearts together in friendship.

Two people are better off than one,
for they can help each other succeed.
If one person falls, the other can reach out and help.

Ecclesiastes 4:9 → 10 NLT

Friendship is the only cement that
will ever hold the world together.

The heartfelt counsel of a friend
is as sweet as perfume and incense.

Proverbs 27:9 NLT

Well Done

There is much satisfaction in work well done,
but there can be no happiness equal
to the joy of finding a heart that understands.

Victor Robinsoll

The gossip of bad people gets them in trouble;
the conversation of good people keeps them out of it.
Well-spoken words bring satisfaction;
well-done work has its own reward.

Proverbs 12:13–14 MSG

Let us begin from this moment to acknowledge
Him in all our ways, and do everything,
whatsoever we do, as service to Him and for His glory,
depending upon Him alone for wisdom,
and strength, and sweetness, and patience.

Hannah Whitall Smith

I would give more for the private esteem and love
of one than for the public praise of ten thousand.

W. E. Alger

Good friend, don't forget all I've taught you;
take to heart my commands. They'll help you
live a long, long time, a long life lived full and well.

Proverbs 3:1-2 MSG

*Well done, good and faithful servant!
You have been faithful with a few things;
I will put you in charge of many things.*

Matthew 25:21 NIV

Do well the little things now and then great things
will come to you by and by, asking to be done.

Persian Proverb

The Rhythm of Love

Let God have you, and let God love you—and don't be
surprised if your heart begins to hear music you've never
heard and your feet learn to dance as never before.

Max Lucado

God knows the rhythm of my spirit and knows
my heart thoughts. He is as close as breathing.

*Come to me. Get away with me and you'll recover
your life. I'll show you how to take a real rest. Walk
with me and work with me—watch how I do it.
Learn the unforced rhythms of grace. I won't lay
anything heavy or ill-fitting on you. Keep company
with me and you'll learn to live freely and lightly.*

Matthew 11:28-30 MSG

From the heart of God comes the strongest rhythm—
the rhythm of love. Without His love reverberating
in us, whatever we do will come across like a noisy
gong or a clanging symbol. And so the work
of the human heart, it seems to me, is to listen for
that music and pick up on its rhythms.

Ken Gire

Then those who sing as well as those
who play the flutes shall say,
"All my springs of joy are in you."

Psalm 87:7 NASB

In waiting we begin to get in touch with the rhythms
of life—stillness and action, listening and decision.
They are the rhythms of God. It is in the everyday
and the commonplace that we learn patience,
acceptance, and contentment.

Richard J. Foster

God's Path

Listen...and be wise, and keep your
heart on the right path.

Proverbs 23:17 NIV

Those who run in the path of God's
commands have their hearts set free.

We can make our plans,
but the LORD determines our steps.

Proverbs 16:9 NLT

They are well guided that God guides.

Scottish Proverb

God's wisdom is always available to help
us choose from alternatives we face, and help
us to follow His eternal plan for us.

Gloria Gaither

Your word is a lamp to my feet and a light for my path.

Psalm 119:105 NIV

Whoever walks toward God one step,
God runs toward him two.

Jewish Proverb

*The very steps we take come from GOD;
otherwise how would we know where we're going?*

Proverbs 20:24 MSG

God's Word acts as a light for our paths.
It can help scare off unwanted thoughts in our
minds and protect us from the enemy.

Gary Smalley and John Trent

God's bright sunshine overhead,
God's flowers beside your feet...
And by such pleasant pathways led,
May all your life be sweet.

Helen Waithman

What Lies Within

It is not in the pursuit of happiness that we find
fulfillment, it is in the happiness of pursuit.

Denis Waitley

He who pursues righteousness and love finds life,
prosperity and honor.

Proverbs 21:21 NIV

A span of life is nothing. But the man or woman who
lives that span, they are something. They can fill that
tiny span with meaning, so its quality is immeasurable,
though its quantity may be insignificant.

Chaim Potok

And I pray that you...will have the power to understand
the greatness of Christ's love—how wide and how
long and how high and how deep that love is....
Then you can be filled with the fullness of God.

Ephesians 3:18-19 NCV

What lies behind us and what lies before us are
tiny matters compared to what lies within us.

Ralph Waldo Emerson

*You're blessed when you're content with
just who you are—no more, no less. That's the
moment you find yourselves proud owners of
everything that can't be bought.*

Matthew 5:5 MSG

Vision looks inwards and becomes duty.
Vision looks outwards and becomes aspiration.
Vision looks upwards and becomes faith.

Stephen Samuel Wise

Your eyes are windows into your body.
If you open your eyes wide in wonder and belief,
your body fills up with light.

Matthew 6:23 MSG

Purity

Our hearts are not made happy by words alone.
We should seek a good and pure life, setting our minds
at rest and having confidence before God.

Thomas à Kempis

*Create in me a pure heart, O God, and renew
a steadfast spirit within me. Do not cast me from
your presence or take your Holy Spirit from me.
Restore to me the joy of your salvation
and grant me a willing spirit, to sustain me.*

Psalm 51:10-12 NIV

The secret of purity is God. Get a pure heart from God
and you can be supremely happy no matter what the
circumstances and no matter what is going on around you.

Billy Graham

The pure in heart live transparently...no guile,
no hidden motives.

Charles R. Swindoll

He who has clean hands and a pure heart...
will receive blessing from the LORD.

Psalm 24:4-5 NIV

Love is not getting, but giving. Not a wild dream of
pleasure and a madness of desire—oh, no—love is
not that! It is goodness and honor and peace and pure
living—yes, love is that and it is the best thing in the
world and the thing that lives the longest.

Henry Van Dyke

Dreams Fulfilled

Lift up your eyes. Your heavenly Father waits
to bless you—in inconceivable ways to make
your life what you never dreamed it could be.

Anne Ortlund

Those who hope in the LORD
will renew their strength.
They will soar on wings like eagles;
they will run and not grow weary,
they will walk and not be faint.

Isaiah 40:31 NIV

God created us with an overwhelming desire to soar....
He designed us to be tremendously productive and
"to mount up with wings like eagles," realistically
dreaming of what He can do with our potential.

Carol Kent

*I came so they can have real and eternal life,
more and better life than they ever dreamed of.*

John 10:10 MSG

God is not an elusive dream or a phantom to chase, but a
divine person to know. He does not avoid us, but seeks us.
When we seek Him, the contact is instantaneous.

Neva Coyle

I'll lead you to buried treasures,
secret caches of valuables—
Confirmations that it is, in fact, I, God...
who calls you by your name.

Isaiah 45:3 MSG

The human heart has hidden treasures,
In secret kept, in silence sealed—
The thoughts, the hopes, the dreams, the pleasures,
Whose charms were broken if revealed.

Charlotte Brontë

Destiny

Recognizing who we are in Christ and aligning our
life with God's purpose for us gives a sense of destiny....
It gives form and direction to our life.

Jean Fleming

*You guide me with your counsel,
leading me to a glorious destiny.*

Psalm 73:24 NLT

No matter what some people may say, you are important.
You. God loves even the weirdest parts of you. He knows
that those parts have value you may not yet understand.

Marilyn Jansen

Live out your God-created identity. Live generously and
graciously toward others, the way God lives toward you.

Matthew 5:48 MSG

God has a purpose for your life
and no one else can take your place.

I believe that nothing that happens
to me is meaningless, and that it is good
for us all that it should be so....
As I see it, I'm here for some purpose.

Dietrich Bonhoeffer

Everything has already been decided.
It was known long ago what each person
would be. So there's no use arguing
with God about your destiny.

Ecclesiastes 6:10 NLT

When the world around us staggers from lack of direction,
God offers purpose, hope, and certainty.

Gloria Gaither

Made for Joy

Our hearts were made for joy. Our hearts were made
to enjoy the One who created them. Too deeply
planted to be much affected by the ups and downs of
life, this joy is a knowing and a being known by our
Creator. He sets our hearts alight with radiant joy.

May the righteous be glad and rejoice before God;
may they be happy and joyful.

Psalm 68:3 NLT

If one is joyful, it means that one is faithfully living
for God, and that nothing else counts; and if one gives
joy to others, one is doing God's work.
With joy without and joy within, all is well.

Janet Erskine Stuart

The joy of the Lord is your strength.

Nehemiah 8:10 NKJV

Live for today but hold your hands open to tomorrow.
Anticipate the future and its changes with joy. There is
a seed of God's love in every event, every circumstance,
every unpleasant situation in which you may find yourself.

Barbara Johnson

Satisfy us in the morning with your unfailing love,
that we may sing for joy and be glad all our days.

Psalm 90:14 NIV

Joy is the holy fire that keeps our purpose warm
and our intelligence aglow.

Helen Keller

In His Likeness

*The God of the universe—the One who created
everything and holds it all in His hand—
created each of us in His image, to bear His
likeness, His imprint. It is only when Christ
dwells within our hearts, radiating the pure light
of His love through our humanity, that we discover
who we are and what we were intended to be.*

Wendy Moore

In the very beginning it was God who formed
us by His Word. He made us in His own image.
God was spirit and He gave us a spirit so that He could
come into us and mingle His own life with our life.

Madame Jeanne Guyon

Made in His image, we can have real meaning,
and we can have real knowledge through
what He has communicated to us.

Francis Schaeffer

For in Him all the fullness of Deity dwells in bodily
form, and in Him you have been made complete.

Colossians 2:9-10 NASB

God looks at the world through the eyes of love. If we,
therefore, as human beings made in the image of God
also want to see reality rationally, that is, as it truly is,
then we, too, must learn to look at what we see with love.

Roberta Bondi

Happy and Thankful

It is not how much we have, but how much we enjoy,
that makes happiness.

Charles H. Spurgeon

In him our hearts rejoice,
for we trust in his holy name.
May your unfailing love rest upon us, O LORD,
even as we put our hope in you.

Psalm 33:21 - 22 NIV

Sometimes our thoughts turn back toward a corner
in a forest, or the end of a bank, or an orchard
powdered with flowers, seen but a single time...
yet remaining in our hearts...is not to be forgotten, a
feeling we have just rubbed elbows with happiness.

Guy de Maupassant

*Devote yourselves to prayer with
an alert mind and a thankful heart.*

Colossians 4:2 NLT

Our inner happiness depends not on what
we experience but on the degree of our
gratitude to God, whatever the experience.

Albert Schweitzer

I will bless the LORD at all times:
His praise shall continually be in my mouth.

Psalm 34:1 NKJV

Maybe we could spend a moment at the end of each
day and decide to remember that day—whatever may
have happened—as a day to be grateful for.
In so doing we increase our heart's capacity to choose joy.

Henri J. M. Nouwen

The Goodness of God

The goodness of God is infinitely more wonderful
than we will ever be able to comprehend.

A. W. Tozer

I am still confident of this: I will see the goodness of the
LORD in the land of the living. Wait for the LORD;
be strong and take heart and wait for the LORD.

Psalm 27:13–14 NIV

All that is good, all that is true, all that is beautiful,
all that is beneficent, be it great or small, be it perfect
or fragmentary, natural as well as supernatural,
moral as well as material, comes from God.

John Henry Newman

How great is your goodness, which you have stored
up for those who fear you, which you bestow in the
sight of men on those who take refuge in you.

Psalm 31:19 NIV

*Our God is so wonderfully good,
and lovely, and blessed in every way that
the mere fact of belonging to Him is enough
for an untellable fullness of joy!*

Hannah Whitall Smith

Open your mouth and taste, open your eyes
and see—how good GOD is. Blessed are you who run
to him. Worship God if you want the best; worship
opens doors to all his goodness.

Psalm 34:8-9 MSG

God Listens

You can talk to God because God listens.
Your voice matters in heaven. He takes you
very seriously. When you enter His presence,
the attendants turn to you to hear your voice.
No need to fear that you will be ignored. Even if you
stammer or stumble, even if what you have to say
impresses no one, it impresses God—and He listens.

Max Lucado

*I love the LORD because he hears my voice and
my prayer for mercy. Because he bends down to
listen, I will pray as long as I have breath!*

Psalm 116:1-2 NLT

God listens in compassion and love, just like we
do when our children come to us. He delights
in our presence. When we do this, we will
discover something of inestimable value.
We will discover that by praying we learn to pray.

Richard J. Foster

This is the confidence we have in approaching God:
that if we ask anything according to his will, he hears us.
And if we know that he hears us—whatever we ask—
we know that we have what we asked of him.

1 John 5:14–15 NIV

We come this morning—
Like empty pitchers to a full fountain,
With no merits of our own,
O Lord—open up a window of heaven...
And listen this morning.

James Weldon Johnson

New Every Morning

Ah, Hope! what would life be, stripped of your
encouraging smiles, that teach us to look behind
the dark clouds of today, for the golden beams
that are to gild the morrow.

Susanna Moodie

Weeping may remain for a night,
but rejoicing comes in the morning.

Psalm 30:5 NIV

Hold on, my child! Joy comes in the morning!
Weeping only lasts for the night....
The darkest hour means dawn is just in sight!

Gloria Gaither

O LORD, be gracious to us; we long for you.
Be our strength every morning,
our salvation in time of distress.

Isaiah 33:2 NIV

When morning gilds the skies,
My heart awaking cries:
May Jesus Christ be praised!

Joseph Barnby

Then your light will break forth like the dawn,
and your healing will quickly appear; then your
righteousness will go before you, and the glory
of the LORD will be your rear guard.

Isaiah 58:8 NIV

That is God's call to us—simply to be people who are
content to live close to Him and to renew the kind of life
in which the closeness is felt and experienced.

Thomas Merton

The faithful love of the LORD never ends!
His mercies never cease.
Great is his faithfulness;
his mercies begin afresh each morning.

Lamentations 3:22-23 NLT

Love Never Fails

Love is patient, love is kind and is not jealous;
love does not brag and is not arrogant, does not
act unbecomingly; it does not seek its own, is not
provoked, does not take into account a wrong suffered,
does not rejoice in unrighteousness, but rejoices with
the truth; bears all things, believes all things, hopes
all things, endures all things. Love never fails.

1 Corinthians 13:4–8 NASB

God is the sunshine that warms us,
the rain that melts the frost and waters
the young plants. The presence of God is a climate
of strong and bracing love, always there.

Joan Arnold

An instant of pure love is more precious to God...
than all other good works together.

John of the Cross

Show us your unfailing love, O LORD,
and grant us your salvation.

Psalm 85:7 NIV

The King of love my Shepherd is,
Whose goodness faileth never;
I nothing lack if I am His,
And He is mine forever.

Sir Henry Williams Baker

[God's] heart is the most sensitive and tender of all. No
act goes unnoticed, no matter how insignificant or small.

Richard J. Foster

Experience Hope

You are not here merely to make a living.
You are here in order to enable the world to live
more amply, with greater vision, with a finer spirit of
hope and achievement. You are here to enrich the world,
and you impoverish yourself if you forget the errand.

Woodrow Wilson

May the God of hope fill you with all joy
and peace as you trust in him, so that you may
overflow with hope by the power of the Holy Spirit.

Romans 15:13 NIV

Hope is a state of mind, not of the world. Hope,
in this deep and powerful sense, is not the same
as joy that things are going well, or willingness
to invest in enterprises that are obviously
heading for success, but rather an ability
to work for something because it is good.

Havel Vaclav

"Hope" is the thing with feathers—
That perches in the soul—
And sings the tune without the words—
And never stops—at all.

Emily Dickinson

I pray for you constantly, asking God, the glorious Father
of our Lord Jesus Christ, to give you spiritual wisdom and
insight so that you might grow in your knowledge
of God. I pray that your hearts will be flooded with
light so that you can understand the confident hope
he has given to those he called—his holy people
who are his rich and glorious inheritance.
I also pray that you will understand the incredible
greatness of God's power for us who believe him.

Ephesians 1:16-17 NLT

HOPE is the ability to hear the music of the future....
FAITH is having the courage to dance to it today.

PETER KUZMIC

Faith Adventure

Faith sees the invisible, believes the incredible,
and receives the impossible.

In this you greatly rejoice, though now for a little while
you may have had to suffer grief in all kinds of trials.
These have come so that your faith—of greater worth
than gold, which perishes even though refined by fire—
may be proved genuine and may result in praise, glory and
honor when Jesus Christ is revealed. Though you have
not seen him, you love him; and even though you do not
see him now, you believe in him and are filled with an
inexpressible and glorious joy, for you are receiving the
goal of your faith, the salvation of your souls.

1 Peter 1:6-7 NIV

Faith means you want God and want to want
nothing else.... In faith there is movement
and development. Each day something is new.

Brennan Manning

There will always be the unknown.

There will always be the unprovable.

But faith confronts those frontiers with a thrilling leap.

Then life becomes vibrant with adventure!

Robert Schuller

With God all things are possible.

Mark 10:27 NKJV

God wants us to approach life, full of expectancy
that God is going to be at work in every situation
as we grow in our faith in Him.

Colin Urquhart

Faith is not a sense, not sight, not reason,
but a taking God at His Word.

Faith Evans

A Life Worthwhile

I wish you humor and a twinkle in the eye.
I wish you glory and the strength to bear its burdens.
I wish you sunshine on your path and storms to season
your journey. I wish you peace—in the world in which
you live and in the smallest corner of the heart where
truth is kept. I wish you faith—to help define your
living and your life. More I cannot wish you—
except perhaps love—to make all the rest worthwhile.

Robert A. Ward

His divine power has granted to us everything pertaining
to life and godliness, through the true knowledge of Him
who called us by His own glory and excellence.

2 Peter 1:3 NASB

Real joy comes not from ease or riches
or from the praise of people,
but from doing something worthwhile.

Wilfred Grenfell

*I consider everything a loss
compared to the surpassing greatness
of knowing Christ Jesus my Lord.*

Philippians 3:8 NIV

What makes life worthwhile is having a big
enough objective, something which catches our
imagination and lays hold of our allegiance....
What higher, more exalted, and more compelling
goal can there be than to know God?

J. I. Packer

A Wonderful Future

Those who build the future are those who know
that greater things are yet to come, and that they
themselves will help bring them about.

Melvin J. Evans

*Look at those who are honest and good, for a
wonderful future awaits those who love peace.*

Psalm 37:37 NLT

Learn from the past, work for the present,
and plan for the future.

Janette Oke

Guide me in your truth and teach me...
my hope is in you all day long. Remember, O LORD,
your great mercy and love, for they are from of old.

Psalm 25:5-6 NIV

You can never change the past. But by the
grace of God, you can win the future.
So remember those things which will
help you forward, but forget those things
which will only hold you back.

Richard C. Woodsome

Let the beauty of the LORD our God be upon
us, and establish the work of our hands for us.

Psalm 90:17 NKJV

Each day can be the beginning
of a wonderful future.

I have it all planned out—plans to take
care of you, not abandon you, plans to give
you the future you hope for.

Jeremiah 29:11 MSG

At Home

Make your home in me just as I do in you. In the
same way that a branch can't bear grapes by itself
but only by being joined to the vine, you can't
bear fruit unless you are joined with me. I am the
Vine, you are the branches. When you're joined
with me and I with you, the relation intimate
and organic, the harvest is sure to be abundant.
Separated, you can't produce a thing.... But if
you make yourselves at home with me and my
words are at home in you, you can be sure that
whatever you ask will be listened to and acted
upon.... I've loved you the way my Father has
loved me. Make yourselves at home in my love.

John 15:4–7 MSG

God is always present in the temple of your heart...His home. And when you come in to meet Him there, you find that it is the one place of deep satisfaction where every longing is met.

This is and has been the Father's work from the beginning—to bring us into the home of His heart.

George MacDonald

How lovely are Your dwelling places, O LORD of hosts! My soul longed and even yearned for the courts of the LORD; my heart and my flesh sing for joy to the living God.... For a day in Your courts is better than a thousand outside.

Psalm 84:1-2, 10 NASB

Contentment

Contentment is not the fulfillment of what you want,
but the realization of how much you already have.

Godliness with contentment is great gain.
For we brought nothing into the world,
and we can take nothing out of it. But if we have
food and clothing, we will be content with that.

1 Timothy 6:6-8 NIV

If we are cheerful and contented,
all nature smiles...the flowers are more fragrant,
the birds sing more sweetly, and the sun,
moon, and stars all appear more beautiful,
and seem to rejoice with us.

Orison Swett Marden

God wants us to be present where we are. He invites us to see and to hear what is around us and, through it all, to discern the footprints of the Holy.

Richard J. Foster

I have learned to be content in whatever circumstances I am. I know how to get along with humble means, and I also know how to live in prosperity; in any and every circumstance I have learned the secret of being filled and going hungry, both of having abundance and suffering need. I can do all things through Him who strengthens me.

Philippians 4:11 – 13 NASB

Know by the light of faith that God is present, and be content with directing all your actions toward Him.

Brother Lawrence

Friendship with God

Friendship with God is a two-way street.... Jesus said that
He tells His friends all that His Father has told Him;
close friends communicate thoroughly and make a transfer
of heart and thought. How awesome is our opportunity to
be friends with God, the almighty Creator of all!

Beverly LaHaye

Become friends with God;
he's already a friend with you.

1 Corinthians 5:20 MSG

God's friendship is the unexpected joy
we find when we reach His outstretched hand.

Janet L. Smith

Steep yourself in God-reality, God-initiative,
God-provisions.... You're my dearest friends!
The Father wants to give you the very kingdom itself.

Luke 12:31-32 MSG

I have called you friends, for all things
that I have heard from My Father
I have made known to you.

John 15:15 NASB

We can look to God as our Father. We can have a
personal sense of His love for us and His interest in us,
for He is concerned about us as a father is concerned for
his children.... Incredible as it may seem, God wants our
companionship. He wants to have us close to Him. He
wants to be a father to us, to shield us, to protect us, to
counsel us, and to guide us in our way through life.

Billy Graham

In His Hand

The mystery of life is that the Lord of life
cannot be known except in and through the
act of living. Without the concrete and specific
involvements of daily life we cannot come to know
the loving presence of Him who holds us in the palm
of His hand.... Therefore, we are called each day
to present to our Lord the whole of our lives.

Henri J. M. Nouwen

*Behold, I have inscribed you
on the palms of My hands.*

Isaiah 49:16 NASB

I'm a little pencil in the hands of a loving God
who is writing a love letter to the world.

Mother Teresa

God promises to keep us in the palm of His hand, with
or without our awareness. God has already made a space
for us, even if we have not made a space for God.

David and Barbara Sorensen

Do not fear, for I am with you; do not be dismayed,
for I am your God. I will strengthen you and help you;
I will uphold you with my righteous right hand.

Isaiah 41:10 NIV

The God who holds the whole world in His hands
wraps Himself in the splendor of the sun's light
and walks among the clouds.

That Hand which bears all nature up
Shall guard His children well.

William Cowper

Good Gifts

Gratitude consists in a watchful, minute attention
to the particulars of our state, and to the multitude of
God's gifts, taken one by one. It fills us with
a consciousness that God loves and cares for us,
even to the least event and smallest need of life.

Henry Edward Manning

All God's gifts are right in front of you
as you wait expectantly for our Master Jesus....
And not only that, but God himself is right
alongside to keep you steady and on track.

1 Corinthians 1:7-8 MSG

To be grateful is to recognize the Love of God in
everything He has given us—and He has given us
everything. Every breath we draw is a gift of His love,
every moment of existence is a gift of grace.

Thomas Merton

For who do you know that really knows you,
knows your heart? And even if they did,
is there anything they would discover in you that
you could take credit for? Isn't everything you have
and everything you are sheer gifts from God?

1 Corinthians 4:7 MSG

As God loves a cheerful giver,
so He also loves a cheerful taker,
who takes hold on His gifts with a glad heart.

John Donne

Let them give thanks to the LORD
for his unfailing love...for he satisfies the thirsty
and fills the hungry with good things.

Psalm 107:8–9 NIV

Source of Wonder

Dear Lord, grant me the grace of wonder. Surprise me,
amaze me, awe me in every crevice of Your universe....
Each day enrapture me with Your marvelous things
without number. I do not ask to see the reason for it all;
I ask only to share the wonder of it all.

Abraham Heschel

May our lives be illumined
by the steady radiance
renewed daily,
of a wonder,
the source of which
is beyond reason.

Dag Hammarskjöld

I would maintain that thanks are the highest
form of thought, and that gratitude
is happiness doubled by wonder.

G. K. Chesterton

*I will give thanks to the LORD with all my
heart; I will tell of all Your wonders.
I will be glad and exult in You;
I will sing praise to Your name, O Most High.*

Psalm 9:1-2 NASB

As we grow in our capacities to see and enjoy the joys
that God has placed in our lives, life becomes a glorious
experience of discovering His endless wonders.

Show the wonder of your great love,
you who save by your right hand
those who take refuge in you from their foes.
Keep me as the apple of your eye;
hide me in the shadow of your wings

Psalm 17:7-8 NIV

Be Unique

What we do is less than a drop in the ocean. But if that drop were missing, the ocean would lack something.

Mother Teresa

Let's just go ahead and be what we were made to be, without enviously or pridefully comparing ourselves with each other, or trying to be something we aren't.

Romans 12:6 MSG

When we live life centered around what others like, feel, and say, we lose touch with our own identity. I am an eternal being, created by God. I am an individual with purpose. It's not what I get from life, but who I am, that makes the difference.

Neva Coyle

All kinds of things are handed out by the Spirit, and to all kinds of people! The variety is wonderful.

1 Corinthians 12:4 MSG

Do what you know best:
if you're a runner, run;
if you're a bell, ring.

Ignas Bernstein

For we are God's masterpiece. He has created
us anew in Christ Jesus, so we can do the good things
he planned for us long ago.

Ephesians 2:10 NLT

Remember that you are needed.
There is at least one important work to be done
that will not be done unless you do it.

Charles Allen

O LORD, you are our Father.
We are the clay, you are the potter;
we are all the work of your hand.

Isaiah 64:8 NIV

One of Jesus' specialties is to make
somebodies out of nobodies.

Henrietta Mears

Keep Knocking

Perseverance is a great element of success.
If you only knock long enough and loud enough
at the gate, you are sure to wake up somebody.

Henry Wadsworth Longfellow

*Ask and it will be given to you;
seek and you will find; knock and the door
will be opened to you. For everyone who asks
receives; he who seeks finds; and to him who
knocks, the door will be opened.*

Matthew 7:7-8 NIV

Most of the important things in the world have been
accomplished by people who have kept on trying when
there seemed to be no hope at all.

Dale Carnegie

We also rejoice in our sufferings, because we know that
suffering produces perseverance; perseverance, character;
and character, hope. And hope does not disappoint us,
because God has poured out His love into our hearts.

Romans 5:3–5 NIV

Hope means hoping when things are hopeless, or it is no
virtue at all.... As long as matters are really hopeful,
hope is mere flattery or platitude; it is only when
everything is hopeless that hope begins to be a strength.

G. K. Chesterton

As you know, we consider blessed those who have
persevered. You have heard of Job's perseverance
and have seen what the Lord finally brought about.
The Lord is full of compassion and mercy.

James 5:11 NIV

I Will Carry You

We know certainly that our God calls us to a
holy life. We know that He gives us every grace,
every abundant grace; and though we are so
weak of ourselves, this grace is able to carry us
through every obstacle and difficulty.

Elizabeth Ann Seton

*Listen to me..you whom I have upheld
since you were conceived, and have carried
since your birth. Even to your old age and
gray hairs I am he, I am he who will sustain
you. I have made you and I will carry you;
I will sustain you and I will rescue you.*

Isaiah 46:3 – 4 NIV

They travel lightly whom God's grace carries.

Thomas à Kempis

He will feed His flock like a shepherd: He will gather
the lambs with His arm, and carry them in His bosom,
and gently lead those who are with young.

Isaiah 40:11 NKJV

I could see only one set of footprints,
So I said to the Lord, "You promised me,
Lord, that if I followed You,
You would walk with me always...."
The Lord replied,
"The times when you have seen only one set of footprints
Is when I carried you."

Ella H. Scharring-Hausen

An Invitation

If you have ever:
questioned if this is all there is to life...
wondered what happens when you die...
felt a longing for purpose or significance...
wrestled with resurfacing anger...
struggled to forgive someone...
known there is a "higher power" but couldn't define it...
sensed you have a role to play in the world...
experienced success and still felt empty afterward...
then consider Jesus.

A great teacher from two millennia ago, Jesus of Nazareth, the Son of God, freely chose to show our Maker's everlasting love for us by offering to take all of our flaws, darkness, death, and mistakes into His very body (1 Peter 2:24). The result was His death on a cross. But the story doesn't end there. God raised Him from the dead and invites us to believe this truth in our hearts and follow Jesus into eternal life

If you confess with your mouth that Jesus is Lord and believe in your heart that God raised him from the dead, you will be saved. —ROMANS 10:9 NLT